30 Days to Greatness
Self Discipline

By *Lucia Georgiou*

A bit about me and a quick thank you

About the 30 Days to Greatness series:

Hi there, my name is Lucia, and I'd like to tell you a bit about myself before you jump into the books. I am a competitive physique athlete and have won female fitness physique titles in the UK. I can speak 4 languages and at present I am a director and/or partner to several different online companies. It has not always been this way. I am originally from Slovakia and lived in shall we say......... A less economically developed area in probably what you would consider extremely poor living conditions. Luckily, the library nearby had the internet and I saw an opportunity to better my life in England, UK. I had no knowledge of how to speak English, but figured I would learn when I got there. I left in 2010 and the rest is history. Therefore, I know how important having energy, confidence, discipline and the right mindset can be and I'm going to share my thoughts with you.

I didn't want a bunch of books that are long winded boring and get left half way through. I want succinct, easy to digest ACTIONABLE material that can IMPACT peoples lives QUICKLY. So I have decided to make them CHALLENGES. 30 day challenges as you have probably figured out by the title. Each day you are given tasks to complete. Over 30 days the aim is to have a strong grasp of what it is the book sets out to teach. Whether it be to learn a new language, persuade and influence, boost confidence and energy or any other of the topics, you can achieve big things in short periods of time. My vision is to have participation across social media where upon people share what they have achieved in short periods of time and inspire others to do the same. So keep an eye out on facebook, twitter, Instagram, tumblr and pinterest.

Let's get people achieving!

So thanks a lot for purchasing the book or series. I wish you the very best and hope you get what you came looking for.

I would also like to thank Diana Melnic and Vlad Melnic for their superb contributions to the series of books who have provided great support and knowledge throughout the entire project.

Table of Contents

Introduction 1

Day 1 to 5 - Know Your Dark Side 5

Day 1 - Negativism 6

Day 2 - Cynicism 7

Day 3 - Defeatism 9

Day 4 - Delayism 11

Day 5 - Escapism 12

Day 6 - Choose your Goal 14

Day 7 - Make Things Clear 16

Day 8 - The Plan 18

Day 9 - The Barriers 20

Day 10 - The Guilt-Free Reward List 21

Day 11 - Introducing Mindfulness 22

Day 12 - A Powerful Routine 24

Day 13 - Getting excited! 25

Day 14 - Reverse escalation 27

Day 15 - Monitor Your Progress 29

Day 16 - Learning to Let Go 31

Day 17 - A Word for Perseverance 32

Day 18 - The Fear of Failure 33

Day 19 - The Fear of Success 35

Day 20 - A Time for Reflection 37

Day 21 - The Private Praise 38

Day 22 - Situational Relaxation 40

Day 23 - The Power of Visualization 42

Day 24 - The Long-Term Self-Contract 43

Day 25 - Affirmations 44

Day 26 - Plan B 46

Day 27 - Maintenance – The Opposite Hand 47

Day 28 - Maintenance – Your Posture 48

Day 29 - The Risk of Willpower Depletion 49

Day 30 - Back to the Goal Sheet 51

Conclusions 52

A Cheeky Request 54

30 Days to Greatness Series 55

30 DAYS TO GREATNESS: SELF-DISCIPLINE

Introduction

What is self-discipline? What does it mean to lack it? Why do you think you're not as disciplined as you would like? Is it because

- you manage your time poorly?

- you lack organizational skills?

- you're not motivated enough?

- procrastination is your greatest enemy?

- you're just too lazy?

What many people don't realize is that all of these issues, which they see as causes of poor self-discipline, are actually symptoms. Are you confronting one or more of them? If you're reading this book, then you've decided it's time for a change of significant proportions, a change that might take only 30 days to implement, but that will last you for a lifetime. Your conviction is admirable, but to undergo such a change, you must first understand what self-discipline is and what it is not.

Self-discipline is *not*:

- a personality trait that some people have and others don't.

- using willpower to force yourself into action.

On the contrary, self-discipline is:

- a skill that *anyone can learn and train.*

- becoming aware of your conscious or subconscious resistance to action and using different techniques *to overcome,* but *not to crush* that resistance.

Our personalities are complex and never unilateral. We are made up of desires, emotions, needs, fears, intellect, thoughts, memories, imagination and several other different, but connected elements. None of these fully represent us and sometimes, one side of us feels differently than another. Oftentimes, this can create a conflict between emotions and intellect, between fear and desire, between desires and needs.

Self-discipline, then, is the learnable skill to monitor and manage the various sides of our personalities so that, instead of being paralyzed by inner conflict, we can move towards a consciously chosen goal through the collaboration of all our psychological elements.

Why do we *really* lack self-discipline? That's probably because, as a generation and culture, we are *spoiled*. This is not to say, by any means, that we all live comfortable lives, that we're not faced with difficult issues or that our lack of means does not sometimes make us suffer. However, unlike the generations before us, we have been brought up in a world of *instant gratification*. When we need entertainment, we turn on the TV or fire up a PC game. When we feel hungry, we drop by the nearest supermarket. When we want to socialize, we click a few buttons to land on Facebook and see our friends.

In other words, we're used to getting what we need extremely quickly. But our dreams and our ambitions are out of our immediate grasp; and when we have to work on something slow, laborious and difficult, we tend to give up and return to the much-more-familiar TV. It's in our nature!

...and yet, it doesn't make us happy. There comes a time when we need to feel that we have accomplished something more, that we are a part of something more important than ourselves and that, when our time comes, we'll face it without regrets. There comes a time, therefore, when we need self-discipline; because regardless of what our dreams may be, whether they involve career goals, financial success, a happy family, travelling, charity or anything else, self-discipline is the one skill that we cannot succeed without.

There is good news! Beginning with a study conducted in 1994, psychologists have made surprising discoveries about self-discipline. Although our summary here cannot do all this research justice, the main ideas put forth are that

- willpower is finite and can be drained

and

- willpower is like a muscle that can be either atrophied or exercised, practiced and built up.

In other words, no matter how spoiled we've been so far, we can change. We, too, can become like those determined, focused people that we admire. As you go through this life-changing 30 days challenge, remember that what you are doing is exercising your willpower muscle for the long run. Good luck!

Know Your Dark Side

A t the beginning of your journey, perhaps the most important thing to understand is that *there is a part of you that does not want to be self-disciplined.*

Why? We all have a rebellious side to our personalities, an inner child that battles any form of authority at any cost. You might hear yourself thinking:

- Routine will turn me into a slave.

- I will no longer be a fun person.

- I'll lose my freedom, and nothing is worth that price.

In all of these instances, you're dealing with your inner childlike rebel, who ceaselessly works to sabotage your self-discipline efforts. To be successful, you must never try to ignore or crush this part of you, but rather to apply the right techniques to gain its cooperation. For now, you'll spend the following five days learning more about your inner rebel and its mostly subconscious tactics of self-disruption. Here we go!

Negativism

F avourite toxin: *Why bother, when there's already so much wrong in the world?*

Sound familiar? This is one of the most common and most effective ways for your inner rebel to sabotage your efforts. Just as you begin to plan how you'll handle this 30 days program, negative happenings from throughout your life start popping in your head. Everything unpleasant from your environment is suddenly in the spotlight, and what about the fact that our planet is dying and millions of people are starving as we speak? Life begins to look like a drudgery, and what a fitting reward at the end of it!

Your response: As there are bad things in the world, there are also good things. Remember that what you focus on is a matter of attitude. Take today to carefully consider how negativism creeps up in your thoughts. Recognize its favourite lines and write all of them down for later. Over the course of the next month, whenever you feel like quitting, glance over this list and ask yourself: *Do I really want to quit or am I just being negative?*

Cynicism

F avourite toxins: *This is too easy to have any value.*

This is too difficult to complete.

Who came up with all this self-help fluff anyway?

Managed to get rid of negative thoughts? Prepare yourself to be bombarded by cynical remarks from within. The cynical side of you is always inclined to question the value of what you are doing; and guess what? Nothing in life is perfect, so your inner cynic can thrive while finding flaws in everything. Unfortunately, it will make no exception for this self-discipline challenge and will constantly try to point out why it won't work.

Your response: Today, consider how cynicism is affecting your desire to become more self-disciplined. Like before, write down all the cynical statements that come to mind about the program. Then, embrace the fact that neither you, nor this guide can be perfect, so you can never expect perfect results. What you can expect, however, is that at the end of the program, your self-discipline will improve greatly and this will show in all aspects of your life. Trust in your ability to improve, because even recognizing negative self-talk for what it is represents a step forward!

Defeatism

F avourite toxins: *Maybe the program is good, but it surely won't work for me.*

Others might be able to become more disciplined, but I'm different.

I'm not smart enough to understand the program.

I'm too smart to care for lame self-help fluff.

The list can carry on indefinitely, because no one is better than you at pointing out your own perceived flaws. But if you allow your rebellious inner child to dig up feelings of insecurity and low self-esteem, you're likely to either give up on the challenge or go about it so half-heartedly that you'll greatly minimize its benefits.

Your response: After writing down all your self-defeating "arguments" for why you shouldn't even try the 30 day challenge, spend some time considering their validity. Then, acknowledge that these self-discipline tips, some of which have been around for hundreds of years, have worked for thousands of people, all of whom were different in their own way. In the future, whenever you feel like giving in to defeatism, redouble your efforts instead of complaining about your shortcomings. Tell yourself: *Nothing is going to stop me.*

DAY 4

Delayism

Favourite toxins: *I'll do it later.*

I couldn't start on (that new diet) until I (can afford a blender).

I just wouldn't have the time.

...and the delays never stop here; because if you need a blender, then you must save some additional money, and you couldn't possibly do that when the upcoming month is already so strenuous on your credit card. At the end of the day, with one hurdle on top of another standing between you and your original goal, you never get to do what you plan.

Your response: We all have responsibilities, so eliminating delayism is a matter of prioritization. Take today, for instance, to write down all the reasons why you feel you might delay your self-discipline challenge. Then, take each reason in turn and ask yourself whether it is legitimate. *Is it working for you or against you?* During the following month, constantly address this question when you want to delay a self-discipline activity. Remind yourself that in order for these techniques to work, you must actually apply them, rather than just think about them.

DAY 5

Escapism

F avourite toxins: *You don't really need to do all this uncomfortable stuff.*

Why don't you find something to eat instead?

Better yet, why not watch some TV?

To become self-disciplined, you first have to learn more about yourself. To do that, you have to ask yourself some difficult questions. You might feel some anxiety or discomfort as you unearth emotional events or situations that you'd rather leave buried in your subconscious. And that's when your inner rebel will offer you the easy way out – just do something else.

Your response: Spend the day writing down the things you are most likely to treat yourself to in order to escape an uncomfortable task. Notice how you go from one thing to the other and how you initially become distracted from your self-discipline activity. Did you feel any better *after* eating, watching TV, etc. or did these actions only offer a temporary feeling of relief? Acknowledge the fact that in order to achieve progress, you must be resolute and constructively confront your inner emotions and fears. Only then will you realise that while they might feel scary, these past events or future concerns have no actual power over you.

Choose your Goal

Today, it's all about you. What is it that you want to achieve the most? Of course, since you're using this guide, you'd like to become more self-disciplined, but that's a very ample goal. It's easy to lose yourself along the way if you don't know exactly where you're going, and it's also easy to give into defeatism if you try to change too many things at a time.

That is why, to begin with, you're going to focus on *just one goal* – the smaller the better. Ask yourself the following questions, and write down your answers:

- What are my current short-term and long-term goals?

- Which of these goals do I most want to achieve?

- Why do I want to achieve the goal I have chosen? What will I accomplish by it or how will it enhance my life, short- and long-term?

- Is there a figure in my life (a friend, family member, notorious person) that inspires me to achieve this goal? If so, what can I learn from them?

For this and all other writing exercises you practise, be attentive! Try not to write your answers automatically, but rather to focus on each word as you write it down. Then, spend the rest of the day considering the goal you have chosen. Remember that in order for it to come true, you must remind yourself of this goal every day, several times.

Make Things Clear

I t might seem strange to focus on only one, small and very specific goal when you're trying to become self-disciplined in all aspects of your life, but the truth is that willpower is contagious! Trying to change everything you don't like about your life at once is a rookie mistake, and will lead you to exhaust your willpower. On the other hand, relevant research tells us that if you devote yourself to one specific goal, reasonably exercise your "willpower muscle" and experience the taste of success, you'll find it significantly easier to improve in other aspects of your life as well.

But let's not get ahead of ourselves. Today, you're going to turn your goal into something *specific, measurable, attainable, relevant and time-bound*. In other words, a SMART goal. Say, for instance, that your first self-discipline goal is to lose weight. To turn this from vague to SMART, ask yourself the following questions:

- What is my ideal weight?

- Is this the weight I would feel comfortable and healthy with or am I pushing myself because of societal, cultural, emotional or other factors? What is the weight I feel comfortable with?

- In what timeframe do I want to achieve this weight?

- Is the amount of weight I want to lose vs. the amount of time I want to spend a realistic goal? If not, what would be a realistic goal?

If weight loss is not your first self-discipline goal, come up with similar questions. Remember that you are trying to outline a SMART goal, so devise your questions accordingly.

The Plan

Try as hard as you might, you could not overstress the importance of a good plan in any endeavour. There are four main stages in the process of becoming more self-disciplined:

- the decision to act,

- planning and preparation,

- action,

- completion and maintenance.

Each of these stages is essential in its own way and skipping one or more of them can put an end to all of your efforts. Yes, there are techniques you can use in order to become more self-disciplined and yes, there are ways to remain self-disciplined for your entire life. But in the absence of a will to act or a healthy plan to act on, all of these tricks become useless.

Today, therefore, is a very special day. Equip yourself with enough paper, pencils and pens, and get planning! Although we recommend writing your plan by hand, changing it around and then writing it again on clear paper, this is not absolutely necessary; you can use your PC or laptop as well. After writing down your SMART goal, here are a few other things to consider:

- Research your goal and find out how others have achieved it.

- Write down any advice that you feel you could work with. Keep an open mind, but don't force yourself to use techniques you're not comfortable with.

- Try to break down your goal into other, smaller goals.

- Come up with a clear timeline for all of these smaller goals.

- Define your success parameters or, in other words, consider what you must achieve in what amount of time so that you will feel proud of yourself.

- Set time aside for reflection. As you monitor your progress in the future, you'll need a bit of time, every now and then, to turn back to the plan, judge its effectiveness and make any necessary changes.

DAY 9

The Barriers

A ccording to a wide range of studies, planning is guaranteed to help you achieve your goal, regardless of what your goal may be. One of the reasons why this is the case is the fact that planning allows you to anticipate the obstacles you will face and to come up with timely solutions. In doing so, you increase your chances of success and you decrease the likelihood that you will quit on your goal.

Today, therefore, you'll be concentrating on the barriers you expect to face as you attempt to become more self-disciplined. You've already explored some of these likely impediments during the first five days of the challenge, but now it's time to look at yourself more closely and come up with personal reasons why you might decide to quit on self-discipline along the way.

It might be difficult to face some of these personal issues even in theory, but remember to be perseverant. For every obstacle you think about, come up with a solution that you are confident will work for you.

The Guilt-Free Reward List

I f day 9 was difficult to complete, day 10 is meant to be its soothing cure. Yesterday, you had to focus on the difficulties of this challenge, but today is all about rewards, motivation and happy thoughts. After all, *if you're going to put yourself through a difficult task, it's only fair that the recompense should be fitting.* This is why today, you'll be making a list of incentives or things that will keep you motivated throughout the remaining 20 days. These will be your means to negotiate the cooperation of your inner childlike rebel, so come up with as many examples as possible. Although no treat is off limits, remember not to choose rewards that defeat your primary goal!

Once the list is completed, set clear goals to achieve for each treat and spread your treats evenly across the next 20 days. Then, title it *The Guilt-Free Reward List*. This is important, because we usually tend to give ourselves a hard time whenever we decide to reward ourselves. Can I really afford it? Do I really deserve it? These are just some of the self-defeating questions that pop to mind. If an item is on your guilt-free reward list, however, that means that you're meant to enjoy it without any tint of remorse. Remember that!

Introducing Mindfulness

I f done correctly, this day will not only help you become more self-disciplined, but it will indeed change your entire life. Mindfulness, a practice of Buddhist origins that has since lost its religious connotations in the West, is a powerful tool with a fantastic reputation. Some of the benefits of mindfulness include:

- Stress management.

- Improved physical and psychological health.

- Enhanced ability to empathize and connect with others.

- Lower risk of depression and anxiety.

- Better self-discipline.

- Overall happiness.

If this is the first time you hear about mindfulness, then it might sound too good to be true. Fortunately, a great deal of research that can document all of the above benefits is now available. Incorporating mindfulness meditation in your life, for only 20 or 30 minutes a day, can lead to drastic improvement, which is why you should spend day 11 of your self-discipline challenge on becoming more acquainted with this practice.

Firstly, you'll have to find a mindfulness guide that suits you and browse through its opening pages. Secondly, you should write down your personal plan in terms of mindfulness meditation, and maybe even try it out a little, if you have the extra time.

A Powerful Routine

Whether your goal is to lose weight, get ahead in your career, volunteer more, make more time for your loved ones or anything else that requires self-discipline, routine is your best friend. Although this may seem perplexing, even when your goal is to become more spontaneous, routine can help you achieve it.

The reason for this is twofold. To begin with, a good routine can help you go about your day more efficiently, and even though you might not believe it now, you'll be surprised by the amount of time you can save if you stay focused on your real goals. Moreover, when you incorporate the habit you wish to learn into a routine, you'll find that it becomes easier to practice. Use this day to consider the aspect of your life where you want to apply more self-discipline and to come up with a relevant routine.

Remember that if you are trying to give up a harmful habit, extinguishing this habit will never work. Instead, you must identify its trigger and its reward, and then find a different habit that can satisfy them.

DAY 13

Getting excited!

T oday, you'll first focus on the distinction between self-discipline and willpower. To put it simply:

- Willpower is your ability to do something when you don't want to do it. It is a short-term burst against internal resistance.

- Self-discipline represents your long-term fidelity to how you envision your ideal self. Unlike simply persevering in the moment, it implies a daily self-directness in your actions and the different facets of your personality.

Although willpower is important, it is also limited and can easily be drained. The more you force yourself to exercise your willpower in the short-term, the less likely you are to become more self-disciplined in the long run. If you've ever put yourself on a diet, then you probably know all about this.

So what does this mean for your challenge? It means that you have to get excited! When you look at those self-disciplined people that you have chosen as models, do you believe they lead the lives they do by constantly forcing themselves? That is as impossible for them as it would be for you. They can be as self-disciplined as they are because they enjoy what they are doing. If you're going to achieve long-term success, then you must also learn to find the joy and thrill in your goals and routines. Spend some time considering this and writing down your results! The aim of the exercise is to get you to rely much less on temporary willpower and more on your internal motivation, so that you can easily avoid burnout.

DAY 14

Reverse escalation

You've been preparing a long time, you're motivated and you're ready to put everything into practice. But when you wake up in the morning on the first day when you should implement your new habit or routine, you just can't get yourself to do it. Or you do get to it, but you feel like quitting halfway through. You beat yourself down and you believe that everything you've done so far has been nothing more than a waste of time.

We propose an alternative. It's called *reverse escalation* and it is based on research claiming that the most difficult part about practicing a routine is actually getting started. Whenever you feel like you just get can't out of bed because you have to work (for example), make a deal with yourself to work for only five minutes. Similarly, if you're already practicing your routine, but you feel like quitting too early, ask yourself to hold out for just another five minutes. Soon enough, "just five minutes" will seem like an easy task and you'll be able to ask yourself for six, and so on. Essentially, you'll be exercising your "willpower muscle", while also getting things done.

From this day forward, we advise that, with a few minor exceptions, you practice your chosen routine towards achieving your specific goal. In addition to this, don't forget to set aside a few minutes every day in order to complete the exercises designed for the remaining duration of the challenge.

Monitor Your Progress

To be successful in any endeavour, you have to be able to evaluate yourself and adjust your routines accordingly. And to conduct a meaningful self-evaluation, you must constantly monitor your progress. Although you'll be doing this for the first time on day 15, monitoring yourself should not be a one-time activity, but rather a habit that you can practice at least every other day. With your goal sheet and initial plan in front of you, ask yourself the following questions:

- Are my routines still relevant for my goal?

- Am I on the right track towards achieving my goal or have I fallen behind?

- Is there anything holding me back from practicing my routines? If so, how can I improve on this issue?

- How have I dealt with the problems I had originally anticipated?

- What problems do I anticipate in the future and how will I solve them?

- Am I still motivated? If not, what changes can I make in my reward system to become motivated again?

Remember that what you are trying to achieve through this self-discipline challenge is meant to last for a lifetime, so don't rush it. If you've fallen behind, don't worry. You can always reschedule and set new timeframes for your goals, without giving into either delayism or defeatism.

DAY 16

Learning to Let Go

N obody is perfect, and nobody is perfectly self-disciplined. In every attempt at self-discipline, there will be bumps along the way, and that's alright. In every diet, there will be the occasional forbidden snack, just like in every fitness program, there will be some disappointing days of inactivity. To achieve lasting results, you must learn to accept your imperfections.

Today, give yourself a day off, and don't be afraid! Trust that you will be able to pick up your challenge right where you left it. Why do this now? Because some failures are inevitable, and whether we like it or not, sooner or later, we must confront them. This day is a chance for you to experience all the emotions that come with quitting and still avoid giving up in the long run. Defeatism and the "all or nothing" attitude will be your greatest enemy today, as well as in any day when you skip on your routines, but don't let it get the best of you. Tell yourself that even though today did not go as planned, tomorrow will. And that's ok.

DAY 17

A Word for Perseverance

I t's always difficult to resume a practice if, for whatever reason, you've skipped on it even once. After day 16, there's no better time to learn about perseverance than today.

If yesterday has gone well for you, then you should have no problem whatsoever in returning to the self-discipline challenge. If, on the other hand, you've spent yesterday with doubts and thoughts of quitting, then it might seem more difficult to get back to your goal today than it was when you first began. Should this be the case, spend today considering the importance of perseverance.

Indeed, it seems that even with all the new techniques we have to get a habit going, perseverance remains the most effective method. It might not feel like it right now, but maintaining a habit for at least 30 to 60 days will eventually turn it from drudgery to normality. In other words, if you manage to be consistent throughout the entire month, by the end of it, your chosen practice will require close to no willpower to accomplish. Remember that!

DAY 18

The Fear of Failure

As you carry on through the challenge, you'll be confronted with all kinds of obstacles, some of which we've already discussed. Today, you'll be exploring the fear of failure and how it can affect your degree of self-discipline.

To put it simply, we all connect failure to humiliation, especially because we are brought up in a culture that ingrains this equivalence in our minds. Naturally, we wish to avoid humiliation, and sometimes this means that we cannot fully commit to a goal. We subconsciously tell ourselves that if we never try, we can never fail. But to become more disciplined, a strong commitment is necessary.

That's why today, you'll be exploring and hopefully resolving your fear of failure. Take a few minutes to write down three past experiences that you perceived as failures or mistakes. Feel free to go as far back into your past as you can remember, even down to your childhood. Make sure that the three experiences you chose are the most embarrassing and humiliating you can recall. This might feel uncomfortable at first, but by writing them down, you'll be giving these experiences a concrete form and, in the process, give yourself the chance to confront them fairly, rather than allow them to haunt your subconscious like ghosts.

The Fear of Success

A lthough we often forget this, success is a double-edged sword. On a conscious level, we're usually so enthralled with the good side of success that we tend to forget the bad. On a subconscious level, however, we fear the negative side-effects of success, sometimes to such a degree that we even work against ourselves and our goals.

Here are just a few reasons why you might fear success:

- You believe you don't deserve to be successful.

- You think that being successful will make others see you with a more critical eye.

- You fear that success will make you lonely and make other resent you.

- You fear that your success will make someone close to you suffer.

- You believe success means too much responsibility, as well as the end of spontaneity and fun.

Spend today asking yourself why you might fear success. Like yesterday, take about 15 minutes to write about three experiences that were successful, but that also created problems for you. Go as far into your past as you can recall, and don't forget to be specific. This might show you why you feel the way you do about success and, as a result, help you overcome your fears.

DAY 20

A Time for Reflection

R emember day 15 and the questions you asked yourself with the purpose of monitoring your progress? Today, you'll be undergoing the same exercise, with a few additional minutes of reflection.

For example, you can take a few minutes to look over your guilt-free rewards list. Is success on the list? When we undertake a project, we often get distracted by all kinds of palpable rewards and we forget that feeling successful is one of the best motivators. As you reflect on your journey so far, consider everything you have accomplished. Is it not easier to stick to your routines now than it was 20 days ago? If the answer is yes, then this is a significant accomplishment. But if the answer is no, don't feel discouraged! Remember that perseverance is one of your most effective tools, and that you can always adjust your initial plan to resolve your issues.

The Private Praise

Having come a long way from the beginning of this challenge, you might sometimes find it difficult to keep up the good work. Whether you're making great progress or you feel like you're not doing enough, what you learn today will help you stay motivated.

Private praise is a technique you can apply *immediately* following any small, positive thought, feeling or action, regardless of how insignificant it may seem. Tell yourself:

- Congratulations! You did it!

- It makes me feel good to get this done.

- Good going!

- Good work!

- Nicely done!

- You can do it!

- Hang in there!

- Don't give up!

Do not attempt to use the opposite of private praise as punishment for failure, because you'll only hurt yourself in the long run. If something goes wrong, don't call yourself stupid or lazy. Instead, tell yourself:

- So I slipped, but it wasn't a big deal. Next time, I'll do better!

Keep up this kind of self-talk on a regular basis, regardless of how small you feel your progress is, and you'll be working psychological wonders. As you praise yourself, remember to smile, so that your subconscious understands that you are proud of yourself.

Situational Relaxation

A s you've already noticed, the techniques you've been learning over the past few days have had the purpose to help you maintain your self-discipline routines even when you no longer feel like it. Today, you'll be learning about situational relaxation, a similar technique that is especially useful when dealing with consumptive behaviours (like smoking, drinking, etc.).

Situational relaxation is based on the assumption that, if you were able to stop for one moment and think about a certain negative behaviour before actually putting it into practice, you'd be able to see all the rationalizing, minimizing and justifying you use in order to motivate that behaviour. Thus, you'd give yourself another tool in preventing it. Here's how it works:

- Take a few deep breaths and slow your breathing.

- Tell yourself: *I am completely relaxed.*

- Tighten and then relax your major muscle groups, one at a time. Begin with your facial muscles.

- Take a minute to really allow your body to relax.

- Then, start asking yourself a few "Why?" questions. For example: *Why do I think that completing this task would be so painful? Why do I really want to eat that chocolate right now? Why am I responding this way?*

- In a relaxed, but firm manner, counterargument your initial answers and focus on the immediate reward you will give yourself after completing the task.

- Still in a relaxed state, take a few actions towards your task. Whenever you feel an avoidance thought or behaviour creeping up, replace it with self-discipline affirmations.

- Actually begin your task, but remember to remain relaxed. If you've managed to begin the task, the hardest part is already over!

The Power of Visualization

At one time or another, we're all confronted with a task we dread – an upcoming exam, the first day on a new diet, that postponed visit to the dentist. To complete this task against our wishes, we're usually required to strain our "willpower muscle" to the point of depletion. That's why today, you'll be practicing visualization and learning how to harness its power to your advantage. When used effectively, visualization can strengthen your commitment, increase your confidence, validate your abilities and reduce the influence of self-defeating thoughts.

But perhaps the best part about visualization is that it is so simple to apply! One week or a few days *before* you have to tackle that dreadful task, take a few minutes or even a few seconds every day to visualize yourself completing it. Think of yourself waking up that morning, going through your early routine, preparing yourself for the task and undergoing it accordingly.

The key is to use as many details as possible in order to obtain a vivid mental movie. Think about what you would feel emotionally, but also consider your sense of smell, touch, hearing and sight. Do this as many times as you get the chance!

DAY 24

The Long-Term Self-Contract

T oday, take a moment to consider your progress. How do you feel about your current degree of self-discipline? Have you achieved the goal you had in mind or, in other words, is your routine already a habit or do you still have to use willpower to enforce it? If the latter is your answer, don't worry! There's even more techniques you can use.

One of them is the long-term self-contract that you will outline today. On a blank piece of paper and using your guilt-free rewards list, postulate a few terms that dictate specifically what task you must complete for what reward.

Why is this necessary? Unlike simply thinking about the contract, the act of writing it will involve you in your agreement both psychologically and physiologically, adding more power to your efforts. Give it a try!

Affirmations

This is a technique that you've been using during the entire challenge, but today, you'll make even more specific use of it. If you've heard about affirmations before, then you won't be surprised to know that they can be a very powerful tool in formatting your subconscious mind. Take a look at your initial goal sheet, and then write a relevant affirmation using your name in three different ways. For instance, you can write:

I, Maria, enjoy life without smoking.

You, Maria, enjoy life without smoking.

Maria enjoys life without smoking.

Basically, you'll be writing the same affirmation in the first, second and third person. Remember to keep the affirmation in the present and avoid negatives. *Do not write,* for instance: *I, Maria, do not smoke.* Once you've completed your first set of affirmations, copy it another two times. Then, separate the three sets by breaking the paper you've written them on. Put two of them in two different places where you will see them many times every day, and put the third in your wallet or purse. Every time you remember your affirmation, and at least ten times a day, read it. Whenever you change your goal in the future, change your affirmations as well.

———

Plan B

A lready at day 26, you're drawing near to the end of this challenge. Whether you've mastered your routine and achieved your initial goal or you're still struggling, a plan B will be useful for you in the future. So what do we mean by plan B?

It's a trick that works just as well as incentives – accountability. Tell your friends, your family or/and your loved one about your goal. Let them in on your plans and your progress so far, and ask them for advice. Also ask them to check up on you from time to time! Alternatively, start a simple blog and tell your audience about your struggle or even join a support group in your town.

Accountability will replenish your willpower like few other techniques would. That's why today, you should spend your time either making a few phone calls or setting up a personal self-discipline challenge blog.

Maintenance - The Opposite Hand

A s you probably already know, either from personal experience or your journey over the past 26 days, willpower is a "muscle" that needs regular maintenance. Regardless of how much progress you've made so far, you have to bear this mind if you're going to reap the benefits of the challenge for the rest of your life.

Today, you'll be looking at a simple trick to exercise your "willpower muscle" without risking depletion. As the title above suggests, set one hour during the course of the day and, during that hour, use your opposite hand to complete regular tasks. In other words, if you usually use your right hand, then use your left. The vice-versa applies. Continue to do this every day or at least once every other day in order to keep your willpower in shape.

Maintenance - Your Posture

L ike yesterday, today you'll be trying out a willpower maintenance exercise. This exercise is a great way not only to flex your "willpower muscle", but also to maintain a healthy posture. Because, let's face it, whether we actually work a desk job, we just enjoy spending our time in front of the PC or both, we all tend to sit for a long time during the day. In the long run, this takes its toll on the body.

For this willpower exercise, take a look at a picture of the correct sitting posture. Then, monitor your own posture throughout the day. Whenever you find yourself slouching, pick up your back into a correct position. Easy enough, right? This will not readily deplete your willpower, but it will certainly solicit and exercise it.

The Risk of Willpower Depletion

F inally, on the penultimate day of our self-discipline challenge, we feel that a recap is in order. If you've made it so far, great work! Don't forget to praise yourself for a job well done! But before you do and before you apply these techniques towards a new goal, remember that willpower is a muscle and, like any muscle, it can be overworked. An exhausted willpower muscle is, perhaps, one of the greatest obstacles in the way of long-term self-discipline, which is why we've put together a list of things you can do in order to avoid it:

- Never attempt to crush the rebellious side of your personality, but rather attempt to gain its cooperation.

- Do not force yourself to overcome your resistance to a certain action or routine. Instead, find exciting or positive aspects about it and use as little willpower as possible to achieve it.

- Make use of reverse escalation whenever you implement a new routine.

- Let go of the "all or nothing" attitude and persevere in spite of your shortcomings.

- Be compassionate and patient with yourself.

- Use meditation and visualization whenever you face a difficult task.

- Keep practicing your willpower muscle.

- Reward and praise yourself every small step of the way!

Take today to consider which of these techniques have worked best for you and write them all down. In the future, return to this list whenever you feel that you are using too much of your willpower in the attempt to stay self-disciplined.

Back to the Goal Sheet

C ongratulations on making it to day 30! Really well done! You've completed the self-discipline challenge and, hopefully, you've got a new, stable, positive habit to show for it. After completing your daily routine, take a few moments to reflect on your journey and appreciate how far you have come.

Truly remarkable! But don't mistake this accomplishment for the end of your real self-discipline challenge – life itself. Having accomplished one of your goals, no matter how small, you should find it much easier to return to the goal sheet and follow your larger dreams. Isn't that exciting? With all of these techniques at your disposal, what should you pursue next?

You already know? Well then, this calls for a plan!

Conclusions

There's no feeling quite as empowering as the taste of success. No more than one month ago, you might have thought that nothing could help you change; that nothing could give you the drive you needed to stay motivated long enough to pursue your dreams. Today, you can look at these goals through a new perspective, where everything is possible.

Or maybe, you haven't had as much success with your self-discipline challenge. Perhaps you've quit on your routine several times throughout the 30 days, skipped on some of the exercises and sifted through others without writing them down. In spite of what you might think, this is not a reason to stop trying. Nor is it a reason to beat yourself up with negative self-talk. In fact, you probably already know that *"failure is not defeat unless you stop trying"*. You may not trust this saying at this point, but it is true.

If life involved no failures, then we would never need self-discipline at all. Everything would happen for us, and we would never know the bitterness of defeat. The question is, however, would success remain as precious? Many philosophers agree that experiencing both meagreness and greatness is the very essence of our human nature. This means that, sooner or later, each of us feels disappointed about something. The secret is to have the power to persevere, and what else is self-discipline all about?

What should you do, then, when you let yourself down and the idea of success is too distant to overcome the immediate sense of failure? Trust that, even though you haven't excelled in your journey so far, you have made progress. You have learned more and more techniques to deal with your inner rebel or, at least, you've acquired a new attitude towards it – a new perspective. Ask yourself honestly: *Am I willing to change?*

If the answer is yes, start over.

A Cheeky Request

I f I have helped to motivate, inspire or provide value from the book in anyway. Could I ask a cheeky favor?

Could you leave a review please? I want to help as many people as possible and the reviews will help people make an informed choice

Thanks again for your support!

30 Days to Greatness Series

I f you enjoyed the book and want to learn or achieve more I have listed the rest of the series below. You will find them in the author page or you can simply search the title or '30 Days to Greatness' Also if you enjoy more than 3, maybe you should consider the box set. Check our page for offers.

- Self love

- Self discipline

- Boost confidence and self assertiveness

- Learn a new language

- Persuade and influence

- Weight loss

- Detox

- Boost energy and vitality

- To quit binge eating

- To mindfulness

- To start an online business with Amazon FBA

- To reduce stress

Made in the USA
Monee, IL
26 December 2024